SPEAKING THE WORD OF GOD
IN FIRST PERSON NOUN

Pt. 2

CYNTHIA D. JOHNSON

**SPEAKING THE WORD OF GOD
IN FIRST PERSON NOUN Pt. 2**

Cynthia D. Johnson

All rights reserved. This book or any portion thereof may not be reproduced or used in any manner whatsoever without the express written permission of the publisher except for the use of brief quotations in a book review.
Unless otherwise noted, all scriptures were taken from the King James Version.

**Copyright 2025 C.I. No. 40317420348
ISBN: 979-8-9985264-1-1
Printed in the U.S.A.**

Table of Contents

Dedication 4

Introduction 5

Healing 7

Wealth and Prosperity 14

Emotional Intelligence 22

Living a Godly Life 30

Living by Faith 38

Boldness and Steadfastness 46

The Peace of God 55

Patience to Wait 62

Author's Bio 72

Contact 74

Dedication

This book is round two for those who are learning to speak the word of God in the first-person noun.

Many times, we're speaking God's word in third-person noun, such as "them, they, we, and us," but the word is more effective when we see ourselves in the word and visualize the end of any situation.

As you view the following pages, remember, as you speak the word aloud, it builds your faith to see every situation at its end.

Introduction

When it comes to applying the word of God one must be specific with the words that comes out of your mouth. In the spiritual realm, there are spiritual ears that take to heart everything you say.

James 1:19 instructs us to be "slow to speak, quick to hear, slow to anger." This should be taken to heart, knowing the words you speak has an impact on your world.

The following pages are separated by subjects for the need in your life.

As you read them aloud, allow your voice to become the footprint in the earth, believing what you've said, to see the change in the earth so the Lord can move on your behalf and be glorified through you and in you.

Take the word of God at heart and see yourself healed, delivered, whole and set free from the afflictions, bondages, diseases, and any other stronghold the world of sin has placed in your life since your birth.

I pray these words are a blessing to your life for the seasons that are to come.

HEALING

The word of God states, deliverance is the children's bread. I believe the Lord wants everyone who's called by the name of Jesus should be healed, whole, delivered, and set free.

Sometimes, we open the door to give the enemy a legal seat in our lives, by the things we digest and what we speak.

The following forty scriptures can be declared over your life, and the lives of others for healing, using the first-person noun:

Healing Through God's Word

Isaiah 53:5 – By His stripes, I am healed.

Jeremiah 30:17 – The Lord restores my health and heals my wounds.

Exodus 15:26 – The Lord is my healer; He takes away sickness from me.

Psalms 103:2-3 – The Lord forgives all my sins and heals all my diseases.

Proverbs 4:20-22 – God's Word is life and health to my whole body.

Matthew 8:17 – Jesus bore my sickness and carried my diseases.

3 John 1:2 – I prosper and am in good health, even as my soul prospers.

James 5:15 – The prayer of faith heals me, and the Lord raises me up.

Mark 11:24 – I believe that I receive healing when I pray, and it is mine.

Psalms 147:3 – The Lord heals my broken heart and binds up my wounds.

Healing from Sickness and Disease

Deuteronomy 7:15 – The Lord takes away all sickness from me.

Malachi 4:2 – The Sun of Righteousness arises over me with healing in His wings.

Psalms 30:2 – I cry out to the Lord, and He heals me.

Matthew 9:22 – Jesus says to me, "Your faith has made you well," and I am healed.

Mark 16:17-18 – I lay hands on the sick, and they recover, including myself.

Luke 4:40 – Jesus lays His hands on me, and I am healed.

Acts 10:38 – Jesus heals me because He was anointed to do so.

Isaiah 41:10 – I will not fear, for God strengthens, helps, and upholds me.

Psalms 91:10 – No plague shall come near my dwelling.

2 Chronicles 7:14 – As I humble myself and seek the Lord, He heals my body and land.

Healing for My Mind and Emotions

Romans 12:2 – I am transformed by the renewing of my mind.

2 Timothy 1:7 – God has given me a spirit of power, love, and a sound mind.

Philippians 4:7 – The peace of God guards my heart and mind in Christ Jesus.

Isaiah 26:3 – The Lord keeps me in perfect peace because my mind is stayed on Him.

John 14:27 – Jesus gives me His peace, so I am not troubled or afraid.

Psalms 23:3 – The Lord restores my soul.

1 Peter 5:7 – I cast all my anxiety on Him because He cares for me.

Isaiah 40:31 – As I wait on the Lord, He renews my strength.

Nehemiah 8:10 – The joy of the Lord is my strength.

Psalms 34:17 – When I cry out, the Lord hears and delivers me from all my troubles.

Victory Over Infirmity and Weakness

Romans 8:11 – The Spirit of God gives life to my mortal body.

1 Corinthians 6:19-20 – My body is the temple of the Holy Spirit, and I honor God with it.

Isaiah 58:8 – My healing springs forth speedily.

Psalms 118:17 – I will not die but live and declare the works of the Lord.

Matthew 17:20 – By faith, I command sickness to leave, and it obeys.

Hebrews 10:23 – I hold fast to my confession of faith, for God is faithful.

Job 33:25 – My flesh is renewed and fresher than a child's.

John 10:10 – Jesus gives me life abundantly.

Ephesians 6:10 – I am strong in the Lord and in the power of His might.

Numbers 6:24-26 – The Lord blesses me, keeps me, and gives me peace.

WEALTH AND PROSPERITY

I don't believe that prosperity and wealth should be spoken about more than the word of God that teaches us how to live, but wealth and prosperity is a big part of Christian living.

The word states, God gives us the mind to create wealth. When we think outside of the box of becoming a creative source, we obtain wealth in our hands to fund Kingdom initiatives, events, and are able to sow into those who are in need.

Don't be afraid to say what the Lord says we can have. As you seek the kingdom first, and God's righteousness, He will add to you everything you need.

Deuteronomy 8:18 – I remember the Lord my God, for it is He who gives me the power to create wealth.

Philippians 4:19 – My God supplies all my needs according to His riches in glory by Christ Jesus.

Psalms 23:1 – The Lord is my shepherd; I shall not lack anything.

3 John 1:2 – I prosper in all things and remain in good health, just as my soul prospers.

Proverbs 10:22 – The blessing of the Lord makes me rich, and He adds no sorrow with it.

2 Corinthians 9:8 – God makes all grace abound toward me, so that I always have all sufficiency in all things and an abundance for every good work.

Joshua 1:8 – I meditate on God's Word day and night, and I make my way prosperous and successful.

Malachi 3:10 – As I bring my tithes into the storehouse, the windows of heaven are opened for me, and blessings overflow in my life.

Psalms 1:3 – I am like a tree planted by the rivers of water; I bring forth fruit in season, and everything I do prospers.

Isaiah 48:17 – The Lord teaches me to profit and leads me in the way I should go.

Luke 6:38 – As I give, it is given to me—good measure, pressed down, shaken together, and running over.

Proverbs 3:9-10 – As I honor the Lord with my wealth and first fruits, my barns are filled with plenty, and my vats overflow with new wine.

Deuteronomy 28:2-6 – Blessings overtake me because I obey the Lord my God. I am blessed in the city and blessed in the field.

Ecclesiastes 5:19 – God has given me riches and wealth, and He enables me to enjoy them.

Psalms 112:3 – Wealth and riches are in my house because I fear the Lord.

Isaiah 60:5 – The wealth of the nations shall come to me, and my heart shall rejoice.

Zechariah 9:12 – Today I declare I receive double for every trouble I have faced.

2 Chronicles 20:20 – I believe in the Lord my God, and I am established; I believe His prophets, and I prosper.

Genesis 13:2 – Like Abraham, I am rich in livestock, silver, and gold.

Job 22:28 – I decree a thing, and it is established for me, and light shines on my ways.

Isaiah 61:7 – Instead of shame, I receive a double portion; instead of disgrace, I rejoice in my inheritance.

Psalms 35:27 – The Lord takes pleasure in my prosperity because I serve Him faithfully.

Matthew 6:33 – As I seek first the kingdom of God, all these things are added to me.

2 Corinthians 8:9 – Jesus became poor so that through His poverty, I might become rich.

Romans 8:32 – God, who did not spare His own Son, freely gives me all things.

Genesis 26:12-13 – I sow and reap a hundredfold in the same year, and I continue to prosper until I become very wealthy.

Psalms 145:16 – God opens His hand and satisfies my desires.

Haggai 2:8 – The silver and the gold belong to the Lord, and He blesses me abundantly.

Proverbs 22:4 – By humility and the fear of the Lord, I receive riches, honor, and life.

Deuteronomy 28:11-12 – The Lord makes me abound in prosperity and opens His good treasure to bless all the work of my hands.

Proverbs 8:18 – Riches and honor are with me, enduring wealth, and righteousness.

Mark 10:29-30 – As I give up things for the kingdom, I receive a hundredfold return now in this time.

Joel 2:26 – I eat in plenty and am satisfied, and I praise the Lord my God for His abundant blessings.

Isaiah 65:21-22 – I build houses and dwell in them; I plant vineyards and enjoy their fruit.

Psalms 34:10 – I seek the Lord, and I lack no good thing.

John 10:10 – Jesus came that I may have life and have it more abundantly.

Matthew 7:7-8 – I ask, and it is given to me; I seek, and I find; I knock, and the door is opened for me.

Genesis 39:3 – The Lord is with me, and He makes all that I do prosper in my hands.

Proverbs 13:22 – I leave an inheritance for my children's children, and the wealth of the sinner is stored up for me.

James 1:17 – Every good and perfect gift comes from my Father in heaven.

EMOTIONAL INTELLIGENCE
(A SOUND MIND)

Growing up in the Christian faith, we have to have a sound mind. A sound mind keeps us focused on the things of God. Not having a sound mind, or sound emotions gives space to the devil to wreak havoc on our thoughts. When our minds are sound, our emotions will follow, so that we're not tossed too and from between every wind of doctrine. You're able to discern when the truth presents itself and you'll be able to see through the smoke screen.

1 Corinthians 2:16 - I have the mind of Christ and hold the thoughts, feelings, and purposes of His heart.

Psalms 103:8 - I am slow to anger and rich in love, just as the Lord is.

Colossians 4:6 - I let my words be full of grace, seasoned with salt, so that I know how to answer everyone.

James 1:19 - I am quick to listen, slow to speak, and slow to become angry.

Proverbs 4:23 - I guard my heart diligently, for from it flow the issues of life.

2 Corinthians 10:5 - I take every thought captive to the obedience of Christ, refusing to be controlled by negativity.

2 Timothy 1:7 - I have the spirit of power, love, and a sound mind, not fear or confusion.

Ephesians 4:31-32 - I put away bitterness, rage, anger, slander, and malice, and I choose kindness and compassion.

Ephesians 5:15-16 - I walk in wisdom, making the most of every opportunity.

Philippians 4:7 - The peace of God, which surpasses all understanding, guards my heart and mind in Christ Jesus.

Romans 12:2 - I renew my mind daily with the Word of God, transforming my thoughts and emotions.

Proverbs 31:25 - I am clothed with strength and dignity, and I laugh without fear of the future.

Proverbs 19:11 - I do not allow offense to take root in my heart, for I walk in love and forgiveness.

Ephesians 4:26-27 - I do not let the sun go down while I am still angry, and I give no place to the devil.

1 Peter 5:7 - I cast all my anxiety on the Lord because He cares for me.

Philippians 4:6 - I do not worry about anything, but in everything, I present my requests to God with thanksgiving.

Galatians 5:22-23 - I am filled with the fruit of the Spirit: love, joy, peace, patience, kindness, goodness, faithfulness, gentleness, and self-control.

Proverbs 18:21 - I speak life and not death, blessing and not cursing, over myself and others.

I trust in the Lord with all my heart and do not lean on my own understanding. Proverbs 3:5-6-

Exodus 14:14 - I remain calm and at peace, knowing God fights my battles for me.

Colossians 3:13 - I forgive others just as Christ has forgiven me.

Philippians 4:8 - I meditate on whatever is true, noble, right, pure, lovely, admirable, excellent, and praiseworthy.

Ephesians 4:2 - I am patient with others, bearing with them in love.

Joshua 1:9 - I am strong and courageous, for the Lord is with me wherever I go.

Ephesians 3:17-19 - I am rooted and grounded in God's love, which strengthens me.

Colossians 3:2 - I set my mind on things above, not on earthly things.

John 14:1 - I do not let my heart be troubled, for I trust in God's plan for my life.

Proverbs 3:3-4 - I let love and faithfulness never leave me; I bind them around my neck and write them on my heart.

1 Peter 3:4 - I have a gentle and quiet spirit, which is precious in God's sight.

Romans 12:19 - I do not take revenge but leave room for God's justice.

Ephesians 5:1-2 - I am an imitator of God, walking in love as Christ did.

James 3:17 - I seek wisdom from above, which is pure, peace-loving, gentle, and full of mercy.

Ephesians 6:11 - I put on the full armor of God, standing firm against the enemy's schemes.

Ephesians 4:29 - I speak only about what is helpful for building others up, according to their needs.

Romans 8:14 - I am led by the Spirit, not by my emotions.

Nehemiah 8:10 - I choose joy in all circumstances, for the joy of the Lord is my strength.

Romans 12:21 - I am not overcome by evil, but I overcome evil with good.

Isaiah 40:31 - I wait on the Lord and renew my strength; I mount up with wings like eagles.

Matthew 5:44 - I love my enemies and pray for those who persecute me.

1 John 4:18 - I am being perfected in love, and perfect love drives out fear.

LIVING A GODLY LIFE

Living a godly life is key in today's world. If you love God, you'll obey all what the word tells us to do. There are so many who are calling themselves Christians, but living as the world lives.

Obeying the world of God puts a separation between the good and the profane. You might be cast down and ostracized from loved ones and friends, but to know you have eternal life it worth it all.

Psalms 1:1-2 – I do not walk in the counsel of the wicked, nor stand in the way of sinners, nor sit in the seat of mockers. But my delight is in the law of the Lord, and on His law, I meditate day and night.

Matthew 5:6 – I hunger and thirst for righteousness, and I am filled.

Proverbs 21:21 – I pursue righteousness and love, and I find life, prosperity, and honor.

2 Corinthians 5:21 – I am the righteousness of God in Christ Jesus.

Romans 6:13 – I do not offer any part of myself to sin as an instrument of wickedness, but rather I offer myself to God as someone who has been brought from death to life.

Romans 12:1 – I present my body as a living sacrifice, holy and acceptable to God, as my spiritual worship.

1 Peter 1:15-16 – As God who called me is holy, so I am holy in all my conduct.

1 John 3:7 – Because I practice righteousness, I am righteous just as Jesus is righteous.

Proverbs 4:18 – My path is like the morning sun, shining brighter and brighter until the full day.

Psalms 37:23 – The Lord directs my steps and delights in every detail of my life.

Isaiah 32:17 – The fruit of righteousness in my life is peace, quietness, and confidence forever.

Galatians 5:16 – I walk by the Spirit, and I do not gratify the desires of the flesh.

Colossians 3:5 – I put to death whatever belongs to my earthly nature, and I live by the Spirit of God.

Psalms 119:11 - I have hidden God's Word in my heart so that I might not sin against Him.

Hebrews 12:11 - I embrace the discipline of the Lord, knowing that it produces a harvest of righteousness and peace in my life.

Micah 6:8 - I act justly, love mercy, and walk humbly with my God.

Titus 2:11-12 - The grace of God teaches me to say "No" to ungodliness and worldly passions and to live self-controlled, upright, and godly in this present age.

Psalms 84:11 - The Lord is my sun and shield; He bestows favor and honor. No good thing does He withhold from me because I walk uprightly.

Matthew 6:33 - I seek first the kingdom of God and His righteousness, and all these things are added to me.

Romans 8:4 - I do not walk according to the flesh, but according to the Spirit.

James 1:22 - I am a doer of the Word, not just a hearer, deceiving myself.

1 Timothy 6:11 - I flee from sin and pursue righteousness, godliness, faith, love, endurance, and gentleness.

Psalms 34:15 - The eyes of the Lord are on me because I live righteously, and His ears are open to my cry.

Romans 13:14 - I clothe myself with the Lord Jesus Christ and do not think about how to gratify the desires of the flesh.

Ephesians 5:8-9 – I live as a child of light, for the fruit of the light consists in all goodness, righteousness, and truth.

2 Timothy 3:16-17 – The Word of God trains me in righteousness, so I am equipped for every good work.

Psalms 15:2-3 – I walk uprightly and work righteousness; I speak the truth in my heart and do not slander with my tongue.

1 Corinthians 10:31 – Whether I eat or drink or whatever I do, I do it all for the glory of God.

Philippians 2:15 – I shine like a star in the sky as I live blamelessly and purely in this crooked generation.

1 John 2:6 – Because I claim to live in Jesus, I walk as He walked.

Romans 6:18 - I have been set free from sin and have become a servant of righteousness.

Hebrews 13:18 - I am committed to living honorably in all things.

Psalms 23:3 - The Lord restores my soul and leads me in paths of righteousness for His name's sake.

Isaiah 61:10 - I am clothed with garments of salvation and wrapped in a robe of righteousness.

1 Peter 3:12 - The Lord's eyes are on me because I live righteously, and His ears are attentive to my prayers.

Ephesians 6:14 - I stand firm with the belt of truth and the breastplate of righteousness in place.

Psalms 119:105 – God's Word is a lamp to my feet and a light to my path.

Proverbs 10:9 – Because I walk in integrity, I walk securely.

2 Peter 1:5-7 – I make every effort to add to my faith goodness, knowledge, self-control, perseverance, godliness, mutual affection, and love.

1 Thessalonians 5:23 – The God of peace sanctifies me completely, and my whole spirit, soul, and body are kept blameless at the coming of my Lord Jesus Christ.

LIVING BY FAITH

Living by faith is to walk by faith. I think about Abraham who left everything he knew to step out of his comfort zone, and family to walk by what he heard the Lord say.

It takes growth to walk by faith, believing God, even though you cannot see the outcome or may not understand what the Lord is doing in your life. Faith without work is dead!

Doing what the Lord says according to His word is faith. Believe Him and you shall prosper.

Faith in God's Promises

2 Corinthians 5:7 - I live by faith and not by sight.

Romans 4:20-21 - I walk by faith, fully convinced that God will do what He has promised.

Romans 10:17 - My faith comes by hearing the Word of God.

Proverbs 3:5-6 - I trust in the Lord with all my heart and lean not on my own understanding.

Colossians 3:2 - I set my mind on things above, not on earthly things.

Faith in God's Provision

Philippians 4:19 - My God supplies all my needs according to His riches in glory.

Matthew 6:33 - I seek first the kingdom of God, and all I need is added to me.

Psalms 23:1 - The Lord is my Shepherd; I lack nothing.

Deuteronomy 28:3 - I am blessed in the city and blessed in the field.

Deuteronomy 28:13 - I am the head and not the tail; above only and not beneath.

Faith in God's Protection

Isaiah 54:17 - No weapon formed against me shall prosper.

Psalms 91:1 - I dwell in the secret place of the Most High and abide under the shadow of the Almighty.

Psalms 91:7 - A thousand may fall at my side, ten thousand at my right hand, but it will not come near me.

Psalms 46:1 - The Lord is my refuge and strength, a very present help in trouble.

2 Timothy 1:7 - God has not given me a spirit of fear but of power, love, and a sound mind.

Faith in Healing and Health

Isaiah 53:5 - By the stripes of Jesus, I am healed.

Psalms 103:3 - The Lord forgives all my sins and heals all my diseases.

Ephesians 6:10 - I am strong in the Lord and in His mighty power.

Romans 8:11 - The same Spirit that raised Jesus from the dead lives in me and gives life to my body.

Psalms 118:17 - I will not die but live and declare the works of the Lord.

Faith in Overcoming Challenges

Philippians 4:13 - I can do all things through Christ who strengthens me.

Romans 8:37 - In all these things, I am more than a conqueror through Christ.

1 John 4:4 - Greater is He who is in me than he who is in the world.

Philippians 4:6-7 - I will not be anxious about anything, but in everything, I pray with thanksgiving.

James 4:7 - I resist the devil, and he flees from me.

Faith in God's Strength and Power

Nehemiah 8:10 - The joy of the Lord is my strength.

Isaiah 40:31 - I wait on the Lord, and He renews my strength.

Deuteronomy 1:30 - The Lord goes before me and fights my battles.

1 Corinthians 15:58 - I am steadfast, immovable, always abounding in the work of the Lord.

Matthew 19:26 - With God, all things are possible for me.

Faith in Victory and Breakthrough

John 11:40 - I believe, and I see the glory of God.

Mark 11:24 - Whatever I ask in prayer, believing, I receive.

John 16:33 - I walk in victory because Christ has overcome the world.

Romans 5:17 - I reign in life through Jesus Christ.

Hebrews 10:23 - I hold fast to my confession of faith without wavering.

Faith in God's Unchanging Word

Psalms 119:105 - God's Word is a lamp to my feet and a light to my path.

Matthew 24:35 - Heaven and earth may pass away, but God's Word stands forever.

Isaiah 55:11 - God's Word does not return void but accomplishes what He pleases.

Matthew 7:24-25 - I build my life on the solid rock of God's Word.

Romans 5:1 - I am justified by faith and have peace with God through Jesus Christ.

BOLDNESS & STEADFASTNESS

What does it mean to be bold and steadfast in Christ?

Boldness in Christ means to live with unwavering faith, courage, and conviction in your walk. Regardless of the challenges or oppositions, your life stands on faith, integrity, and the love of God.

Boldness allows you to speak the truth in love, stand firm in righteousness, proclaim the gospel of Christ, and trust in God's power within your life.

Being steadfast enables you to stand strong through the storms without distractions or deceptions. You know what you know, and those things you have been taught, you place them in your heart that you do not sin against the will of God.

Steadfastness helps you endure trials, hold on to God's promises, it won't allow you to be swayed by false doctrine, and it provokes you to press toward the mark of a higher calling in Christ.

Boldness

Proverbs 28:1 - I am as bold as a lion, for I am righteous in Christ.

2 Timothy 1:7 - God has not given me a spirit of fear, but of power, love, and a sound mind.

Joshua 1:9 - I am strong and courageous. I will not be afraid or discouraged, for the Lord my God is with me wherever I go.

Acts 4:29 – Lord, grant me boldness to speak Your word without fear.

Ephesians 6:19 – I declare that I open my mouth boldly to proclaim the mystery of the gospel.

Romans 8:31 – If God is for me, who can be against me?

Hebrews 13:6 – The Lord is my helper; I will not be afraid. What can man do to me?

Philippians 1:14 – I am encouraged and emboldened by the Lord to speak His word without fear.

Isaiah 41:10 – I will not fear, for God is with me. I will not be dismayed, for He strengthens and upholds me.

Psalms 27:1 – The Lord is my light and salvation; I will not fear! The Lord is the strength of my life; I will not be afraid!

1 Corinthians 16:13 – I stand firm in the faith, acting courageously and strong.

Psalms 56:3-4 – When I am afraid, I put my trust in God. In Him, I have no fear!

Deuteronomy 31:6 – I am strong and courageous; I will not fear or be in dread, for the Lord my God goes with me.

Micah 3:8 – I am filled with power, justice, and might by the Spirit of the Lord.

Hebrews 10:35 – I do not throw away my confidence, for it will be richly rewarded.

Isaiah 50:7 – Because the Lord helps me, I will not be disgraced. I have set my face like flint, and I will not be put to shame.

Psalms 138:3 – When I call on the Lord, He makes me bold with strength in my soul.

Acts 28:31 – I proclaim the kingdom of God and teach about Jesus Christ with boldness and without hindrance.

Psalms 118:6 – The Lord is on my side; I will not fear. What can man do to me?

Zechariah 4:6 – Not by might, nor by power, but by the Spirit of the Lord, I walk in boldness.

Steadfastness

1 Corinthians 15:58 – I stand firm, immovable, always abounding in the work of the Lord.

Hebrews 12:1-2 – I run my race with endurance, keeping my eyes on Jesus, the author and finisher of my faith.

Psalms 55:22 – I cast my cares on the Lord, and He sustains me; He will never let me be shaken.

James 1:12 – I am blessed as I persevere under trial, for I will receive the crown of life.

Galatians 6:9 – I do not grow weary in doing good, for at the right time, I will reap a harvest if I do not give up.

Philippians 4:13 – I can do all things through Christ who strengthens me.

Colossians 1:23 – I continue in the faith, established and firm, not moved from the hope of the gospel.

Psalms 16:8 – I keep my eyes always on the Lord; with Him at my right hand, I will not be shaken.

Isaiah 26:3 – God keeps me in perfect peace because my mind is steadfast, trusting in Him.

Romans 12:12 – I rejoice in hope, remain patient in affliction, and stay constant in prayer.

Psalms 112:7-8 – I do not fear bad news; my heart is steadfast, trusting in the Lord.

2 Corinthians 4:8-9 – Though I may be hard-pressed on every side, I am not crushed; though perplexed, I do not despair; though persecuted, I am not abandoned.

2 Thessalonians 3:3 – The Lord is faithful; He strengthens and protects me from the evil one.

Psalms 37:23-24 – The Lord makes firm my steps, and even if I stumble, I will not fall, for He upholds me with His hand.

Lamentations 3:22-23 – The steadfast love of the Lord never ceases; His mercies never end.

1 Peter 5:10 – After I have suffered a little while, the God of all grace will restore, confirm, strengthen, and establish me.

2 Chronicles 15:7 – I am strong and will not let my hands grow weak, for my work will be rewarded.

Psalms 31:24 – I am strong, and my heart takes courage as I wait on the Lord.

Hebrews 6:19 – I have this hope as an anchor for my soul, firm and secure.

Matthew 24:13 – I stand firm to the end, and I will be saved.

THE PEACE OF GOD

God's Promise of Peace

John 14:27 – Jesus has given me His peace; I will not let my heart be troubled or afraid.

Isaiah 26:3 – God keeps me in perfect peace because my mind is stayed on Him, and I trust in Him.

Philippians 4:7 – The peace of God, which surpasses all understanding, guards my heart and mind in Christ Jesus.

Colossians 3:15 – The peace of Christ rules in my heart.

2 Thessalonians 3:16 – The Lord of peace Himself always gives me peace and in every way.

Trusting God for Peace

Psalms 29:11 – The Lord gives me strength and blesses me with peace.

Psalms 119:165 – I love God's law, so I have great peace, and nothing causes me to stumble.

Proverbs 3:5-6 – I trust in the Lord with all my heart and do not lean on my own understanding. He directs my paths and gives me peace.

Romans 8:6 – My mind is set on the Spirit, and I have life and peace.

Isaiah 32:17 – The work of righteousness in my life brings peace, quietness, and confidence forever.

Casting My Cares on God

1 Peter 5:7 – I cast all my anxieties on God because He cares for me.

Matthew 11:28-30 – I come to Jesus when I am weary, and He gives me rest for my soul.

Psalms 4:8 – I lie down and sleep in peace because the Lord makes me dwell in safety.

Psalms 55:22 – I cast my burdens on the Lord, and He sustains me; He will never let me fall.

Exodus 33:14 – God's presence goes with me, and He gives me rest.

Overcoming Fear and Anxiety

2 Timothy 1:7 – God has not given me a spirit of fear but of power, love, and a sound mind.

Isaiah 41:10 – I do not fear, for God is with me. He strengthens me, helps me, and upholds me with His righteous hand.

Psalms 23:4 – Even when I walk through the darkest valley, I fear no evil, for God is with me.

Joshua 1:9 – I am strong and courageous; I do not fear because the Lord is with me wherever I go.

Deuteronomy 31:8 – The Lord goes before me, and He will never leave or forsake me; I will not be afraid.

Peace in Difficult Times

John 16:33 – In Jesus, I have peace; though I face trouble in the world, I take heart because He has overcome it.

Psalms 46:10 – I am still and know that God is in control.

Isaiah 43:2 – When I pass through the waters, God is with me; I will not be overwhelmed.

Nahum 1:7 – The Lord is good, a refuge in times of trouble; He cares for me because I trust in Him.

Romans 15:13 – The God of hope fills me with joy and peace as I trust in Him.

Renewing My Mind for Peace

Philippians 4:8 – I fix my mind on what is true, noble, right, pure, lovely, admirable, excellent, and praiseworthy.

Romans 12:2 – I am transformed by the renewing of my mind, and I experience God's perfect will.

Psalms 19:14 – The words of my mouth and the meditation of my heart are pleasing to the Lord.

Isaiah 26:12 – The Lord establishes peace for me and has done all things for me.

Hebrews 12:14 – I pursue peace with all people and live in holiness.

Victory Over the Enemy's Attacks

Psalms 91:1-2 – I dwell in the secret place of the Most High and rest under the shadow of the Almighty.

Ephesians 6:15 – I stand firm with the gospel of peace as part of my spiritual armor.

James 4:7 – I submit to God, resist the devil, and he flees from me.

Romans 16:20 – The God of peace crushes Satan under my feet.

Luke 10:19 – I have authority over all the power of the enemy, and nothing shall harm me.

God's Love and Presence Brings Me Peace

Zephaniah 3:17 – The Lord rejoices over me with singing and quiets me with His love.

Jeremiah 29:11 – God has plans for my welfare, to give me a future and a hope.

Lamentations 3:22-23 – God's mercies are new every morning; great is His faithfulness to me.

1 John 4:18 – Perfect love casts out all fear, and I walk in God's love.

Galatians 5:22-23 – The fruit of the Spirit in my life includes love, joy, and peace.

PATIENCE TO WAIT

Waiting on God's Timing & Trusting Him

Psalms 130:5 - I wait for the Lord; my soul waits, and in His word, I hope.

Proverbs 3:5 - I trust in the Lord with all my heart and lean not on my own understanding.

Psalms 27:13 - I remain confident of this: I will see the goodness of the Lord in the land of the living.

Psalms 27:14 - I wait on the Lord and take heart, for He will strengthen me.

Ecclesiastes 3:1 - I know that for everything there is a season and a time for every purpose under heaven.

Psalms 46:10 - I am still and know that He is God; He will be exalted in the earth.

Ecclesiastes 3:11 - I trust that the Lord makes all things beautiful in His time.

Galatians 6:9 - I do not grow weary in doing good, for in due season I will reap if I do not give up.

Psalms 37:5 - I commit my way to the Lord and trust in Him, and He will act.

1 Corinthians 15:58 - I stand firm, letting nothing move me, as I give myself fully to the work of the Lord.

Strength in Waiting

Isaiah 40:31 - I wait upon the Lord, and He renews my strength. I mount up with wings like eagles.

Lamentations 3:24 - The Lord is my portion; therefore, I wait for Him.

Lamentations 3:25 - The Lord is good to me because I wait for Him and seek Him.

Psalms 37:7 - I rest in the Lord and wait patiently for Him; I do not fret.

James 1:4 - I let patience have its perfect work in me, so I may be mature and complete.

2 Corinthians 5:7 - I walk by faith and not by sight.

Psalms 46:1 - The Lord is my refuge and strength, a very present help in trouble.

1 Peter 5:6 - I humble myself under God's mighty hand so that He may exalt me in due time.

Galatians 5:25 - I keep in step with the Spirit, allowing Him to lead me.

Psalms 62:5 - My soul waits in silence for God alone, for my expectation is from Him.

God's Promises are Sure

Jeremiah 29:11 - I know the plans God has for me—plans to prosper me and not to harm me, plans to give me a future and a hope.

Philippians 1:6 - I am convinced that He who began a good work in me will complete it.

1 Peter 5:7 - I cast my cares on the Lord because He cares for me.

Isaiah 41:10 - I do not fear, for God is with me; He strengthens and helps me.

Hebrews 10:23 - I hold fast to the confession of my hope without wavering, for He who promised is faithful.

Psalms 31:15 - My time is in His hands.

Isaiah 43:19 - God will make a way in the wilderness and rivers in the desert for me.

Romans 8:28 - I believe that all things work together for my good because I love God.

Proverbs 16:9 - I trust in the Lord, and He directs my steps.

Exodus 14:13 - As I wait, I will see the Lord's deliverance.

Joy & Peace in Waiting

Romans 12:12 - I will be joyful in hope, patient in affliction, and faithful in prayer.

Philippians 4:6-7 - I do not grow anxious, but I pray about everything, and God's peace guards my heart.

Psalms 25:3 - I put my trust in the Lord, and I will never be put to shame.

Romans 5:3-4 - I rejoice in hope, knowing that suffering produces perseverance and character.

John 15:7 - I abide in Jesus, and His words abide in me, so my prayers bear fruit.

Hebrews 6:19 - My hope is an anchor for my soul, firm and secure.

Colossians 3:15 - The peace of Christ rules in my heart, and I am thankful.

2 Corinthians 4:16 - I do not lose heart, for though my outer self wastes away, my inner self is renewed daily.

Hebrews 12:2 - I keep my eyes fixed on Jesus, the author and finisher of my faith.

Romans 8:32 - I rest in God's love, knowing He is working behind the scenes for my good.

NOTES

NOTES

NOTES

NOTES

ABOUT THE AUTHOR

Dr. C.D. Johnson

Dr. Cynthia D. Johnson is the creative force behind DSC Publishers, Inc., which has been owned and operated since 2008, began in Central Florida, and is now licensed in Georgia. She has built a team of outsourced vendors over the past 15 years.

She branched out in 2011 to go back to school. After thirty years of graduating High School, she pursued her undergraduate degree in "Early Childhood Development" and a master's in "Human Service

Counseling," focusing on Public Policy & Blended Families. She recently received a Doctoral of Philosophy Degree in Christian ethics & Business Management.

Her company publishes every genre, from children's books to inspirational journals. Her clients mainly consisted of teachers, doctors, and pastors. Erotica books are the exceptions DSC will not publish.

Her educational background affords her, as an author and trainer, the ability to teach book publishing in groups or individual private workshops about the business. Dr. Johnson is a mother of two business-minded daughters, a son-in-law and five grandsons.

CONTACT

If you'd like to reach out with any questions, comments, or to purchase bulk orders and speaking engagements, feel free to contact me at:

support@dscpublishers.com

Social Media

FB @ DSCBookPublishing

www.ingramcontent.com/pod-product-compliance
Lightning Source LLC
Chambersburg PA
CBHW070426080426
42450CB00030B/1520